AFRICAN AMERICAN ANSWER BOOK

HISTORY

CHELSEA HOUSE PUBLISHERS

AFRICAN AMERICAN ANSWER BOOK

Available in Hardcover • 6 Titles

❑	Arts and Entertainment (0-7910-3201-9)	$12.95
❑	Biography (0-7910-3203-5)	$12.95
❑	Facts and Trivia (0-7910-3211-6)	$12.95
❑	History (0-7910-3209-4)	$12.95
❑	Science and Discovery (0-7910-3207-8)	$12.95
❑	Sports (0-7910-3205-1)	$12.95

Available in Paperback • 6 Titles

❑	Arts and Entertainment (0-7910-3202-7)	$3.95
❑	Biography (0-7910-3204-3)	$3.95
❑	Facts and Trivia (0-7910-3212-4)	$3.95
❑	History (0-7910-3210-8)	$3.95
❑	Science and Discovery (0-7910-3208-6)	$3.95
❑	Sports (0-7910-3206-X)	$3.95

Mail to: Chelsea House Publishers, Dept. Mail Order, P.O. Box 914, 1974 Sproul Road, Suite 400, Broomall, PA 19008-0914

Please send me the book(s) I have checked above.

My payment of $_____ is enclosed. (Please add $1.00 per order to cover postage and handling. PA residents add 6% sales tax.)

Method of payment: ❑ Cash ❑ Check ❑ Money Order
  ❑ Discover ❑ VISA ❑ MasterCard

Credit Card Number: _____

Expiration Date: _____

Phone Number: _____

Signature: _____

Please allow 6 weeks for delivery.

Name _____

Address _____

City _____ State _____ Zip _____

AFRICAN AMERICAN ANSWER BOOK

HISTORY

325 QUESTIONS
DRAWN FROM THE EXPERTISE OF
HARVARD'S DU BOIS INSTITUTE

R. S. Rennert

Chelsea House Publishers
New York   Philadelphia

CHELSEA HOUSE PUBLISHERS
EDITORIAL DIRECTOR Richard Rennert
EXECUTIVE MANAGING EDITOR Karyn Gullen Browne
COPY CHIEF Robin James
PICTURE EDITOR Adrian G. Allen
ART DIRECTOR Robert Mitchell
MANUFACTURING DIRECTOR Gerald Levine
ASSISTANT ART DIRECTOR Joan Ferrigno

AFRICAN AMERICAN ANSWER BOOK
SERIES ORIGINATOR AND ADVISER Ken Butkus
ASSISTANT EDITOR Annie McDonnell
DESIGNER John Infantino
PICTURE RESEARCHER Sandy Jones

5 7 9 8 6 4

ISBN 0-7910-3209-4
ISBN 0-7910-3210-8 (pbk.)

PICTURE CREDITS
The Bettmann Archive: pp. 42, 50; Reuters/Bettmann:
p. 39; The Schomburg Center for Research in Black
Culture, New York Public Library, Astor, Lenox and
Tilden Foundations: p. 47; Special Collections, the
Research Libraries, the New York Public Library,
Astor, Lenox and Tilden Foundations: p. 25; Univer-
sity of Chicago Library: p. 10; UPI/Bettmann: pp. 15,
18, 27, 34.

CONTENTS

INTRODUCTION

In creating the BLACK AMERICANS OF ACHIEVEMENT series for Chelsea House Publishers, I was fortunate enough to work closely with Nathan Irvin Huggins, one of America's leading scholars in the field of black studies and director of the W. E. B. Du Bois Institute for Afro-American Research at Harvard University. His innumerable contributions to the books have not only helped to make BLACK AMERICANS OF ACHIEVEMENT an award-winning series, but his expressed commitment to inform readers about the rich heritage and accomplishments of African Americans has encouraged Chelsea House to draw from his work and develop the 325 questions that make up this *African American Answer Book*.

Each of these briskly challenging questions has been designed to stimulate thought and discussion about African American history. The answers highlight either the leading figures of black America or focus on previously unsung yet equally inspiring African American heroes, their achievements, and their legacies.

You can use these questions to test your own knowledge or to stump your friends. Either way, you will find that this *African American Answer Book*—like its companion volumes—is bound to educate as well as entertain.

—R. S. R.

QUESTIONS

1. What famous march helped influence the Voting Rights Act, passed in August 1965?

    a - *March to Selma*
    b - *Chicago Freedom Movement*
    c - *March on Washington*

2. What is a theme of the classic speech delivered by Martin Luther King, Jr., during the March on Washington that drew 250,000 people?

    a - *"Give Us the Ballot"*
    b - *"We Shall Overcome"*
    c - *"I Have a Dream"*

3. (True or False) In 1964, when Martin Luther King, Jr., received the Nobel Peace Prize at age 35, he was the youngest man ever to receive this honor.

4. What civil rights leader and clergyman organized the Poor People's Campaign in Washington, D.C.?

    a - *Jesse Jackson*
    b - *Ralph Abernathy*
    c - *James Meredith*

5. What antislavery newspaper was founded by Frederick Douglass?

    a - *The North Star*
    b - *The Southern Inquirer*
    c - *The Abolitionist*

6. What is the name of the educational institution that was established by Booker T. Washington in 1881?

    a - *Tuskegee Institute*
    b - *Hampton Institute*
    c - *Howard University*

7. (True or False) Ralph Bunche was the first African American official in the U.S. State Department.

8. What famous quote was written by David Bradley?

    a - *"There are no good times to be black in America, but some times are worse than others."*

    b - *"Free at last, free at last, thank God Almighty, we are free at last."*

    c - *"I, too, sing America. I, too, am America."*

9. In what year did the U.S. Congress abolish slavery?

    a - *1796*
    b - *1808*
    c - *1865*

10. (True or False) L. Douglas Wilder was the first African American to be elected governor.

11. What African American was instrumental in the development of the city of Chicago?

    a - *Jean Baptiste Pointe DuSable*
    b - *Paul Cuffe*
    c - *James Beckwourth*

12. Who was the first African American congresswoman from the South?

    a - *Shirley Chisholm*
    b - *Barbara Jordan*
    c - *Maxine Waters*

13. What antislavery activist was nicknamed after Moses, the biblical figure who led his people from servitude to the Promised Land?

    a - *Sojourner Truth*
    b - *Harriet Tubman*
    c - *Frederick Douglass*

14. Who advocated "equality for every man, self defense and self help"?

    a - *Elijah Muhammad*
    b - *Father Divine*
    c - *Malcolm X*

15. Cheyney State, considered the oldest African American college in the United States, was founded in what year?

   a - *1800*
   b - *1837*
   c - *1869*

16. For a month in 1872 in Louisiana, who became the first African American to serve as governor?

   a - *P. B. S. Pinchback*
   b - *James Rapier*
   c - *Blanche Bruce*

17. (True or False) Elijah Muhammad founded the Nation of Islam.

18. What civil rights group was organized on Abraham Lincoln's birthday in 1909 in New York City?

   a - *NAACP*
   b - *SNCC*
   c - *Niagara Movement*

19. Bethune-Cookman, the first four-year, accredited college founded by a woman (Mary McLeod Bethune), is located in what state?

   a - *Mississippi*
   b - *Florida*
   c - *Alabama*

20. Who were the founders of the Black Panther Party?

   a - *Huey P. Newton & Bobby Seale*
   b - *Ralph Abernathy and Martin Luther King, Jr.*
   c - *Malcolm X and Angela Davis*

21. Who was the first African American mayor of a major U.S. city?

   a - *Tom Bradley in Los Angeles*
   b - *Carl Stokes in Cleveland*
   c - *Maynard Jackson in Atlanta*

22. Name two signers of the NAACP charter.

   a - *Jane Addams & William Dean Howells*
   b - *Thurgood Marshall & Martin Luther King, Jr.*
   c - *Booker T. Washington & George Washington Carver*

A fiery, fearless pioneer in the fight for civil rights, Ida B. Wells-Barnett was a journalist and activist whose antilynching crusade helped awaken the conscience of a nation.

23. What African American writes best-selling mysteries, some of President Clinton's favorite books?

    a - *Walter Mosley*
    b - *Toni Morrison*
    c - *Charles Chesnutt*

24. Who was the first African American to preside over a national political convention?

    a - *Barbara Jordan*
    b - *Ron Brown*
    c - *John Roy Lynch*

25. In 1990, Jesse Jackson negotiated the release of nearly 300 hostages held by:

    a - *Iran*
    b - *Libya*
    c - *Iraq*

26. James Farmer was executive director of the:

   a - *Congress of Racial Equality*
   b - *National Association for the Advancement of Colored People*
   c - *Student Nonviolent Coordinating Committee*

27. In 1977, who became the first African American U.S. ambassador to the United Nations?

   a - *Marian Wright Edelman*
   b - *Jesse Jackson*
   c - *Andrew Young*

28. Who was the first African American to be chairman of the Joint Chiefs of Staff, the highest leadership position in the military next to the president?

   a - *Clifford Alexander, Jr.*
   b - *Colin Powell*
   c - *Benjamin O. Davis, Sr.*

29. What successful black businessman worked to establish independent colonies in Africa for freed slaves?

   a - *Benjamin Banneker*
   b - *Nat Turner*
   c - *Paul Cuffe*

30. Who sued a Tennessee railroad for not allowing her to sit in the "Whites Only" first-class car when she had paid for a first-class ticket?

   a - *Rosa Parks*
   b - *Ida B. Wells-Barnett*
   c - *Mary McLeod Bethune*

31. Booker T. Washington was opposed to the founding of what organization?

   a - *United Negro College Fund*
   b - *National Association for the Advancement of Colored People*
   c - *National Negro Business League*

32. Who was the first African American Supreme Court justice?

   a - *Thurgood Marshall*
   b - *Clarence Thomas*
   c - *Constance Baker Motley*

33. In 1964, Carl T. Rowan was named director of the United States:

> **a** - *Postal Service*
> **b** - *Information Agency*
> **c** - *Secret Service*

34. Who founded the Organization of Afro-American Unity?

> **a** - *Marcus Garvey*
> **b** - *Malcolm X*
> **c** - *Bayard Rustin*

35. In 1946 a fifty-cent coin was issued that was the first coin to honor an African American and the first one designed by an African American. Who did it commemorate?

> **a** - *Harriet Tubman*
> **b** - *Booker T. Washington*
> **c** - *Frederick Douglass*

36. What renowned scholar, an expert on African American history and a patron of African American arts, was the first black chosen as a Rhodes scholar?

> **a** - *Carter G. Woodson*
> **b** - *W. E. B. Du Bois*
> **c** - *Alain Locke*

37. Who became the first African American female lawyer in 1872?

> **a** - *Sojourner Truth*
> **b** - *Charlotte E. Ray*
> **c** - *Jane M. Bolin*

38. Approximately how many African Americans fought for the North in the Civil War?

> **a** - *52,000*
> **b** - *189,000*
> **c** - *350,000*

39. Approximately how many African Americans died in the Civil War?

> **a** - *5,000*
> **b** - *70,000*
> **c** - *150,000*

40. Martin Delany, the first major in the U.S. Army, served in what war?

   a - *Civil War*
   b - *Spanish-American War*
   c - *World War II*

41. (True or False) The Mary Church Terrell House in Washington, D.C., was the residence of the first president of the NAACP.

42. What did Carter G. Woodson start in 1926?

   a - *Martin Luther King, Jr., Day*
   b - *Spingarn Awards*
   c - *Negro History Week*

43. Approximately how many African American men and women served their country during World War II?

   a - *Less than 500,000*
   b - *1 million*
   c - *3 million*

44. (True or False) By 1920, Harlem had become the un-official capital of black America, in which 200,000 African Americans lived within an area of 2 square miles.

45. What African American educator also served as an adviser to five U.S. presidents?

   a - *Mary McLeod Bethune*
   b - *Charlotte Forten Grimké*
   c - *Alain Locke*

46. During Reconstruction (1867–77), congressman Thaddeus Stevens offered what strategy for dealing with freed slaves?

   a - *Give each 40 acres and a mule*
   b - *Send them back to Africa*
   c - *Send them to settle the West*

47. Who was the first African American soldier to receive the Congressional Medal of Honor for his outstanding bravery?

   a - *Crispus Attucks*
   b - *William H. Carney*
   c - *Benjamin O. Davis, Sr.*

48. Who was the first African American to win the Nobel Prize for Literature?

    a - *James Baldwin*
    b - *Toni Morrison*
    c - *Alice Walker*

49. (True or False) Constructed in 1857, Tuskegee Institute originated in the oldest campus building built by slave labor.

50. (True or False) Blanche K. Bruce was the first African American senator to serve a full term.

51. Alexander Crummell was a 19th-century:

    a - *Writer*
    b - *Civil rights leader*
    c - *Religious leader*

52. Where did the name "Jim Crow" originate?

    a - *Character in popular minstrel shows of the 19th century*
    b - *Popular whiskey*
    c - *Slave revolt slogan*

53. What landmark Supreme Court ruling required all railroad companies to provide equal accommodations for blacks?

    a - *Mitchell vs. U.S. Interstate Commerce Act*
    b - *Brown vs. Board of Education of Topeka*
    c - *Irene Morgan vs. Commonwealth of Virginia*

54. (True or False) By 1800, more than 5 million slaves had been shipped from Africa to America.

55. The first indentured African servants arrived in Jamestown, Virginia, in what year?

    a - *1619*
    b - *1668*
    c - *1715*

56. (True or False) Slave owners were encouraged to settle in the Carolinas by offers of free land, with the acreage based upon the number of slaves they owned.

A skilled diplomat and expert on race relations, Ralph Bunche held several important posts in the United Nations and received a Nobel Peace Prize for his mediation of the Arab-Israeli conflict.

57. (True or False) The slave voyage to the Americas was known as "the middle passage."

58. What was the name of the ship that made the first voyage from the North American colonies to bring back slaves from Africa?

    a - *Rainbow*
    b - *Phillis*
    c - *Clothilde*

59. In 1990, who was elected mayor of Washington, D.C., becoming the first African American woman mayor of a major U.S. city?

    a - *Anita Hill*
    b - *Carol Moseley-Braun*
    c - *Sharon Pratt Kelly*

60. Who was the first African American to appear on the presidential ballot in all 50 states?

    a - *Jesse Jackson*
    b - *Lenora Fulani*
    c - *Shirley Chisholm*

61. (True or False) The first major slave revolt happened in New York City in 1712.

62. A slave ship called *Clothilde* was the last slave ship to arrive in America. Where did it land?

    a - *Florida*
    b - *Massachusetts*
    c - *Alabama*

63. What was the name of Martin Luther King, Jr.'s first church?

    a - *Dexter Avenue Baptist Church*
    b - *St. Luke's Episcopal Church*
    c - *Our Lady of Hope Catholic Church*

64. Who was the first African American woman to establish and head a bank?

    a - *Madam C. J. Walker*
    b - *Maggie Lena Walker*
    c - *Frances Ellen Watkins Harper*

65. (True or False) Approximately 5,000 blacks served in integrated American units in the revolutionary war.

66. In 1954, the U.S. Supreme Court issued a monumental decision against segregation in public schools in what famous case?

    a - *Plessy v. Ferguson*
    b - *Sacco v. Vanzetti*
    c - *Brown v. Board of Education of Topeka*

67. (True or False) President Lyndon B. Johnson signed into law the Voting Rights Act on August 6, 1965.

68. How old was Martin Luther King, Jr., when he was assassinated?

    a - *29*
    b - *39*
    c - *44*

69. In what year was Martin Luther King, Jr., fatally shot on the balcony of the Lorraine Motel in Memphis?

    a - *1963*
    b - *1968*
    c - *1970*

70. The first workers, both black and white, that the colonists purchased were called:

    a - *Indentured servants*
    b - *Slaves*
    c - *Hired hands*

71. By the turn of the 18th century, Virginians began importing slaves from West Africa at a rate of:

    a - *1,000 per year*
    b - *5,000 per year*
    c - *8,000 per year*

72. (True or False) In *Before the Mayflower,* Lerone Bennett, Jr., estimates that because of a long history of intermarriage and blacks "passing" for white, approximately 20 percent of American whites have black ancestors and 70 to 80 percent of African Americans have white and Native American ancestors.

73. When Cassius Clay converted to the Nation of Islam, he changed his name to:

    a - *El-Hajj Malik El-Shabazz*
    b - *Elijah Muhammad*
    c - *Muhammad Ali*

74. What legislator's eloquent argument for President Nixon's impeachment drew national praise during the Watergate hearings?

    a - *Jesse Jackson*
    b - *Barbara Jordan*
    c - *Maynard Jackson*

75. (True or False) Elijah Muhammad was an African American Muslim leader who called for a separate African American nation.

Jesse Jackson, who emerged as a leader in the nonviolent civil rights protests of the 1960s, has twice run for the Democratic party's nomination for president and continues to play an influential role on the world stage.

76. Who wrote *The Fire Next Time,* a disturbing vision of the destruction that faced American society if it could not solve its racial problems?

    a - *James Baldwin*
    b - *Ralph Ellison*
    c - *Malcolm X*

77. What African American leader became more willing to work with nonviolent civil rights organizations and liberal whites after experiencing a change of heart in Mecca?

    a - *Malcolm X*
    b - *Walter White*
    c - *Stokely Carmichael*

78. (True or False) Sculptor Selma Burke designed the profile of President Franklin D. Roosevelt that appears on the dime.

79. Gabriel Prosser was arrested and executed in 1800 for what reason?

    a - *Organizing a slave revolt*
    b - *Trying to escape to Florida*
    c - *Practicing his religious beliefs*

80. What African American union organizer helped open the door for the U.S. Congress to pass legislation outlawing job discrimination?

    a - *Malcolm X*
    b - *Stokely Carmichael*
    c - *A. Philip Randolph*

81. (True or False) In August 1965, a six-day riot erupted after a conflict between blacks and police in the Watts section of Los Angeles and resulted in 34 people dead, 1,032 injured, 4,000 arrested, and $35 million in property damage.

82. (True or False) By the eve of the Civil War, three-quarters of all the slaves in the United States were involved in the production of cotton.

83. In 1860, approximately 4 million slaves were owned by approximately how many whites?

    a - *100,000*
    b - *385,000*
    c - *1 million*

84. In 1829 *Walker's Appeal* called for:

    a - *Nonviolence in the abolitionist movement*
    b - *Unquestioned acceptance of slavery*
    c - *Any means necessary to fight slavery*

85. Who was the first black woman to lecture on antislavery issues?

    a - *Sojourner Truth*
    b - *Harriet Tubman*
    c - *Maria W. Stewart*

86. Why did thousands of slaves volunteer to fight for England in the American Revolution?

 a - *They were offered freedom*
 b - *They were offered money*
 c - *They were offered land*

87. (True or False) Richard Wright won the National Book Award for *Invisible Man,* becoming the first African American to receive that honor.

88. Maynard Jackson became the first African American mayor of what city?

 a - *Chicago*
 b - *New York*
 c - *Atlanta*

89. What African American civil rights activist founded the African Methodist Episcopal Church?

 a - *Richard Allen*
 b - *Martin Luther King, Jr.*
 c - *Father Divine*

90. What African American revolutionary led colonial forces during the Boston Massacre in 1770, becoming "the first to defy, and the first to die"?

 a - *Crispus Attucks*
 b - *James Beckwourth*
 c - *Paul Cuffe*

91. What leading crusader against lynching founded the first black women's suffrage organization?

 a - *Mary McLeod Bethune*
 b - *Sojourner Truth*
 c - *Ida B. Wells-Barnett*

92. Racist legislation passed in the South, especially during the 1890s, was referred to as:

 a - *The Peculiar Institution*
 b - *Manumission*
 c - *Jim Crow*

93. Approximately how many African Americans migrated from the South to the North in the 1920s and 1930s?

    a - *500,000*
    b - *1 million*
    c - *3 million*

94. (True or False) During the 1920s, the Cotton Club was a vital cultural center for writers, artists, and entertainers in the Hollywood Renaissance.

95. During the 1890s in the South, approximately how often was an African American lynched?

    a - *Once a month*
    b - *Once a week*
    c - *Once every day or two*

96. What were the black soldiers who primarily fought Native Americans in the West after the Civil War called?

    a - *Buffalo Soldiers*
    b - *The Fighting Freedmen*
    c - *The Black Brigade*

97. (True or False) By 1860, approximately 250,000 blacks lived free from slavery.

98. Who was Martin R. Delany?

    a - *An African American nationalist*
    b - *A noted minister*
    c - *A presidential adviser*

99. (True or False) The Ku Klux Klan was active in the South only.

100. (True or False) John Russwurm, editor of the first African American newspaper, argued that it was "a waste of words to talk of ever enjoying citizenship in this country."

101. (True or False) Barney Ford was a founding father of the state of California.

102. (True or False) In 1870, Barney Ford was worth over $250,000 and used his wealth to help educate and provide jobs for newly freed slaves.

103. What famous African American woman dedicated her life to finding her lost family, which had been separated by slave owners?

   a - *Mary Fields*
   b - *Clara Brown*
   c - *Biddy Mason*

104. People who favored the "Back to Africa" idea in the early 1800s were called:

   a - *Rebels*
   b - *Nationalists*
   c - *Colonists*

105. (True or False) Paul Cuffe was a wealthy shipbuilder and landowner.

106. What respected educator did Martin Luther King, Jr., call "my spiritual advisor"?

   a - *Benjamin E. Mays*
   b - *Father Divine*
   c - *Elijah Muhammad*

107. In 1963, the hundredth anniversary of black emancipation, approximately how many racial demonstrations were there?

   a - *5,000*
   b - *10,000*
   c - *25,000*

108. In what year did Black History Month officially begin?

   a - *1956*
   b - *1966*
   c - *1976*

109. (True or False) William S. Whipper advanced the idea of nonviolent protest almost 100 years before Martin Luther King, Jr.

110. Who helped form the American Moral Reform Society, which helped blacks acquire farm land and aided runaway slaves in their escape to Canada?

   a - *Mary McLeod Bethune*
   b - *William S. Whipper*
   c - *Lewis Latimer*

111. Who was the first African American to receive international recognition as a poet and novelist?

    a - *Phillis Wheatley*
    b - *Langston Hughes*
    c - *Paul Laurence Dunbar*

112. In 1855 John M. Langston was the first African American elected to a public office in the United States. In what offices did he serve?

    a - *Town mayor and then state senate*
    b - *Township clerk and then U.S. Congress*
    c - *District attorney and then mayor*

113. How did Barney Ford make his fortune?

    a - *Hotel and restaurant owner*
    b - *Mining*
    c - *Trade merchant*

114. Matthew Henson was famous for:

    a - *Reaching the North Pole first*
    b - *Discovering a pass through the Sierra Nevada*
    c - *Finding the location for the Panama Canal*

115. Who was William Leidesdorff?

    a - *One of the first African American millionaires*
    b - *One of the first African American teachers*
    c - *The first African American judge*

116. (True or False) Booker T. Washington was known as the "Father of Negro History."

117. Dr. Carter G. Woodson started what organization?

    a - *National Association for the Advancement of Colored People*
    b - *Association for the Study of Negro Life and History*
    c - *United Negro College Fund*

118. Who was not an executive director of the National Association for the Advancement of Colored People?

    a - *Benjamin Hooks*
    b - *Roy Wilkins*
    c - *Booker T. Washington*

119. (True or False) The NAACP was the first national, interracial civil rights organization.

120. Who was elected to Congress in 1944 and became the first congressperson to represent the district of Harlem?

  a - *Adam Clayton Powell, Jr.*
  b - *James Weldon Johnson*
  c - *Shirley Chisholm*

121. James Weldon Johnson referred to the racial disturbances in the summer of 1919 as:

  a - *The Black Summer*
  b - *The Red Summer*
  c - *The Burning Summer*

122. Who was the first African American senator in Congress?

  a - *Blanche K. Bruce*
  b - *Hiram Revels*
  c - *Adam Clayton Powell, Jr.*

123. What white abolitionist urged Frederick Douglass to join the attack on Harper's Ferry?

  a - *Jefferson Davis*
  b - *Andrew Jackson*
  c - *John Brown*

124. What U.S. president appointed Frederick Douglass U.S. general counsel to Haiti?

  a - *Benjamin Harrison*
  b - *Grover Cleveland*
  c - *Andrew Jackson*

125. (True or False) President Grover Cleveland asked Frederick Douglass to continue his job in Washington, D.C.

126. Who was the first African American soldier to be awarded the Congressional Medal of Honor in the Vietnam War?

  a - *Milton Olive*
  b - *Colin Powell*
  c - *Ron Brown*

127. Levi Coffin's midwestern operation, which helped slaves to escape, became known as the Underground Railroad's:

  a - *Grand Central Station*
  b - *Nerve Center*
  c - *Central Command*

A versatile educator, columnist, poet, lyricist, lawyer, and diplomat, James Weldon Johnson was a leader of the NAACP who spurred the organization's growth from 9,000 to 100,000 members.

128. Who were influential writers of the Harlem Renaissance?

    a - *Countee Cullen, Langston Hughes, Zora Neale Hurston*

    b - *Paul Laurence Dunbar, Charles Chesnutt, Harriet Adams Wilson*

    c - *James Baldwin, Alice Walker, Chester Himes*

129. Who turned his home into the first black school in Boston?

    a - *Benjamin Banneker*

    b - *Frederick Douglass*

    c - *Prince Hall*

130. Who helped organize the first "Negro Baptist" church in the American colonies in Savannah, Georgia?

    a - *Richard Allen*
    b - *Andrew Bryan*
    c - *Father Divine*

131. Who appointed Thurgood Marshall to the U.S. Supreme Court?

    a - *John F. Kennedy*
    b - *Lyndon B. Johnson*
    c - *Jimmy Carter*

132. Who published *Freedom's Journal,* the first African American newspaper?

    a - *John Russwurm*
    b - *Frederick Douglass*
    c - *Earl Graves*

133. What civil rights leader gave a stirring keynote address at the Poor People's March on Washington shortly after her husband's assassination?

    a - *Betty Shabazz*
    b - *Coretta Scott King*
    c - *Ethel Kennedy*

134. George Monroe and William Robinson were among the first black:

    a - *Pony Express riders*
    b - *Abolitionists*
    c - *Educators*

135. In 1857, the Supreme Court ruled in the *Dred Scott* case that:

    a - *Segregation was unconstitutional*
    b - *Blacks were not U.S. citizens and therefore had no rights*
    c - *Separate facilities were not equal*

136. African Americans were authorized to enlist in the U.S. Navy in what year?

    a - *1861*
    b - *1881*
    c - *1901*

Coretta Scott King, the widow of Martin Luther King, Jr., has become a respected civil rights activist, author, and lecturer in her own right, directing the Martin Luther King, Jr., Center for Non-violent Social Change.

137. What was the significance of the Fourteenth Amendment?

    a - *Abolished slavery*
    b - *Made African Americans citizens*
    c - *Gave African Americans the right to vote*

138. Marian Wright Edelman founded the:

    a - *National Organization of Women*
    b - *Children's Defense Fund*
    c - *National Federation of Afro-American Women*

139. What internationally renowned actor had his U.S. passport revoked for his activities in left-wing unions, the Progressive Party, the Council on African Affairs, and the National Negro Congress?

    a - *Paul Robeson*
    b - *Sidney Poitier*
    c - *Ira Aldridge*

140. In what year did all 50 states recognize Martin Luther King, Jr., Day?

    a - *1973*
    b - *1983*
    c - *1993*

141. Who was the first African American elected to the U.S. House of Representatives?

    a - *Joseph H. Rainey*
    b - *Robert Elliott*
    c - *Robert Smalls*

142. (True or False) Blanche K. Bruce refused an appointment as ambassador to Brazil because slavery was still legal there.

143. Who was the first African American minister ordained in America?

    a - *Father Divine*
    b - *Absalom Jones*
    c - *Richard Allen*

144. Who founded the first African American Masonic lodge?

    a - *Paul Cuffe*
    b - *Prince Hall*
    c - *David Walker*

145. (True or False) On January 15, 1776, the Continental Congress disapproved of George Washington's action of permitting free blacks to enlist in the revolutionary army.

146. In 1777, what state was the first to abolish slavery?

    a - *Massachusetts*
    b - *Delaware*
    c - *Vermont*

147. (True or False) The second settler in what is now known as the state of Alabama was a black man who was with Hernando de Soto's exploratory expedition.

148. Who was the first black born in colonial America at Jamestown, Virginia?

    a - *Absalom Jones*
    b - *William Tucker*
    c - *Andrew Bryan*

149. In 1641, what was the first colony to recognize slavery as a legal institution?

    a - *Massachusetts*
    b - *Pennsylvania*
    c - *Virginia*

150. (True or False) Gwendolyn S. King was the first African American to hold the position of Commissioner of Social Security.

151. Harold Washington became what city's first African American mayor?

    a - *Detroit*
    b - *Los Angeles*
    c - *Chicago*

152. Carol Moseley-Braun was the first African American woman elected to the U.S.:

    a - *Supreme Court*
    b - *Congress*
    c - *Senate*

153. What United Nations diplomat negotiated a historic settlement between Israel and the surrounding Arab states?

    a - *Ralph Bunche*
    b - *Walter White*
    c - *Andrew Young*

154. Who was the first former Black Panther Party member elected to Congress?

    a - *Bobby Seale*
    b - *Bobby Rush*
    c - *Fred Hampton*

155. What African American said, "The content of one's character is the important thing, not the color of one's skin"?

  a - *Frederick Douglass*
  b - *W. E. B. Du Bois*
  c - *Martin Luther King, Jr.*

156. Dr. Charles Drew revolutionized the use of blood banks and blood plasma, helping to save thousands of lives during what war?

  a - *World War I*
  b - *World War II*
  c - *Vietnam War*

157. (True or False) Macon B. Allen was the first African American lawyer formally admitted to the Bar Association when he passed the examination in Massachusetts in 1845.

158. Who was the recipient of the first Spingarn Award?

  a - *Frederick Douglass*
  b - *Ernest Everett Just*
  c - *James Weldon Johnson*

159. What athlete bolstered racial pride in the early 1900s by beating the "Great White Hope"?

  a - *Joe Louis*
  b - *Jack Johnson*
  c - *Jesse Owens*

160. Thomas Petersen was the first African American to vote in the United States. What amendment gave him this right to vote?

  a - *Thirteenth*
  b - *Fourteenth*
  c - *Fifteenth*

161. (True or False) Jazz saxophonist John Coltrane could improvise four chords in a song, playing as many as 1,000 notes a minute.

162. What classic book, published by William Still in 1872, contains a historical account of fugitive slaves?

    a - *The Escape*
    b - *Underground Railroad*
    c - *Narrative of a Slave*

163. (True or False) Booker T. Washington was born a free man in Franklin County, Virginia, in 1856.

164. (True or False) The *Dred Scott* decision by the U.S. Supreme Court condemned Jim Crow laws.

165. Who led the famous raid on Harper's Ferry in October 1859 in an attempt to free and arm slaves in the area?

    a - *Nat Turner*
    b - *John Brown*
    c - *Dred Scott*

166. (True or False) The Civil Rights Act of March 1875 provided for equal accommodations without discrimination for blacks in public places. The Supreme Court, however, ruled the act unconstitutional, affirming the discriminatory public opinion of that time.

167. (True or False) Henry O. Flipper was the first African American graduate from West Point.

168. What was the name of the famous speech delivered by Booker T. Washington at the Cotton Exposition in Atlanta?

    a - *"Atlanta Compromise"*
    b - *"I've Been to the Mountain Top"*
    c - *"I Have a Dream"*

169. (True or False) Alice Walker won the American Book Award and the Pulitzer prize for *The Temple of My Familiar*.

170. How long did the Montgomery bus boycott, led by Martin Luther King, Jr., last?

    a - *Six weeks*
    b - *Six months*
    c - *One year*

171. Who was Joel E. Spingarn?

    a - *President of the NAACP*
    b - *U.S. Congressman*
    c - *A presidential adviser*

172. (True or False) The *Chicago Defender,* founded in 1905 by Robert Abbott, became the most influential and militant black newspaper.

173. Crystal Bird Fauset became the first African American woman legislator in 1938. She was elected to the:

    a - *U.S. Congress*
    b - *U.S. Senate*
    c - *Pennsylvania State House of Representatives*

174. In 1939 who was appointed the first African American woman judge in the United States?

    a - *Jane M. Bolin*
    b - *Carol Moseley-Braun*
    c - *Charlotte Ray*

175. What was the significance of the 1944 U.S. Supreme Court ruling of *Smith vs. Allwright*?

    a - *Banned the "white primary" that prevented blacks in the South from voting*
    b - *Upheld the "white primary" that prevented blacks in the South from voting*
    c - *Ruled that states must provide equal educational facilities*

176. The first military ship named after an African American was called the:

    a - *S.S. Booker T. Washington*
    b - *S.S. Frederick Douglass*
    c - *S.S. G. W. Carver*

177. Constance Baker Motley, an NAACP lawyer who won the case of James Meredith against the University of Mississippi, went on to become:

    a - *The first woman executive secretary of the NAACP*
    b - *The first African American president of the Bar Association*
    c - *The first African American woman federal judge*

178. Who performed on Broadway an acclaimed dramatic interpretation of the events surrounding the 1992 Los Angeles riots?

    a - *James Earl Jones*
    b - *Anna Deavere Smith*
    c - *Denzel Washington*

179. The Supreme Court unanimously declared, "In the field of public education the doctrine of 'separate but equal' has no place" in what year?

    a - *1954*
    b - *1959*
    c - *1896*

180. What was significant about the slave ship *Amistad*?

    a - *Controlled by slave mutineers*
    b - *Last slave shipment to United States*
    c - *First slave shipment to United States*

181. What constitutional amendment prohibited slavery throughout the United States?

    a - *Thirteenth*
    b - *Fourteenth*
    c - *Fifteenth*

182. (True or False) President Lincoln issued an "eye-for-an-eye" order stating that the Union would shoot a Confederate prisoner for every black prisoner that the Confederates shot.

183. What allowed slave hunters the right to retrieve escaped slaves?

    a - *Plessy v. Ferguson decision*
    b - *Twelfth Amendment*
    c - *Fugitive Slave Act*

184. What did Pompey Lamb do to help aid the colonists in the American Revolution?

    a - *Led black troops*
    b - *Spied*
    c - *Exhibited expert marksmanship*

185. (True or False) Senator Blanche K. Bruce once said, "I have made an issue of every single situation in which our people were denied their rightful share of participation."

A spellbinding public speaker, Malcolm X transcended a criminal past and Nation of Islam rivalries to become one of the nation's most impassioned advocates for black self-determination and racial justice.

186. Which of the following was NOT a former president of the Southern Christian Leadership Conference?

    a - *Martin Luther King, Jr.*
    b - *Ralph Abernathy*
    c - *Angela Davis*

187. What famous photojournalist also directed the movies *Shaft, Sounder,* and *Cotton Comes to Harlem*?

    a - *Sidney Poitier*
    b - *Wallace Houston Terry II*
    c - *Gordon Parks*

188. What African American was the first cultural adviser to the Peace Corps?

    a - *Harry Belafonte*
    b - *Katherine Dunham*
    c - *Dizzy Gillespie*

189. What law prohibited slavery north and west of the 36-30 parallel within the Louisiana Purchase territory?

    a - *Thirteenth Amendment*
    b - *Missouri Compromise*
    c - *Compromise of 1850*

190. (True or False) Lemuel Haynes was a white preacher who had a black congregation in 1753.

191. Who was the first African American member of a presidential cabinet?

　　a - *Robert Weaver*
　　b - *Thurgood Marshall*
　　c - *Colin Powell*

192. Harriet Tubman made 19 trips into the South and helped free approximately how many slaves?

　　a - *175*
　　b - *200*
　　c - *300*

193. Who was the first African American to be named U.S. Surgeon General?

　　a - *Louis Sullivan*
　　b - *Faye Wattleton*
　　c - *Joycelyn Elders*

194. Who earned the nicknames "the little man's lawyer" and "Mr. Civil Rights" for his work on behalf of the poor and minorities?

　　a - *Charles Hamilton Houston*
　　b - *Thurgood Marshall*
　　c - *L. Douglas Wilder*

195. In November 1967 Carl Stokes and Richard Hatcher were elected to what office?

　　a - *Governor*
　　b - *Senator*
　　c - *Mayor*

196. What politician attempted to physically block two black students from integrating the University of Alabama in 1963?

　　a - *Senator Jesse Helms*
　　b - *Governor George Wallace*
　　c - *Governor Orval Faubus*

197. W. E. B. Du Bois left America in 1961 and settled in what country?

　　a - *France*
　　b - *Haiti*
　　c - *Ghana*

198. What do Roy Wilkins, Benjamin Chavis, and Benjamin Hooks have in common?

   a - *All have been executive secretary of the NAACP*
   b - *All are militant black nationalists*
   c - *All went to Morehouse College*

199. Who was the first African American astronaut in space?

   a - *Mae Jemison*
   b - *Guion Bluford, Jr.*
   c - *Ronald McNair*

200. What did the Powell amendment do?

   a - *Ordered busing of schoolchildren to integrate schools*
   b - *Denied blacks the right of assembly*
   c - *Denied federal funds to any state that practiced segregation*

201. In the 1980s many college students and political activists urged colleges and companies to divest. What were they aiming to accomplish?

   a - *To support affirmative action*
   b - *To pass updated civil rights regulations*
   c - *To withdraw U.S. investments in South Africa to protest apartheid*

202. Hyram S. T. Bennett, an African American chef in the mid-1800s, may have been the first to make the:

   a - *Chocolate chip cookie*
   b - *Peanut butter and jelly sandwich*
   c - *Potato chip*

203. In what year did A. Philip Randolph organize the sleeping car porters' union?

   a - *1901*
   b - *1925*
   c - *1941*

204. (True or False) Dr. Mary Church Terrell was the first African American to serve on the Washington, D.C., Board of Education.

205. In what year was the Missouri Compromise passed by Congress?

    a - *1820*
    b - *1857*
    c - *1877*

206. In what year was the Fugitive Slave Law passed?

    a - *1850*
    b - *1863*
    c - *1900*

207. What did security guard Frank Wills discover in 1972?

    a - *Major robbery attempt at Fort Knox*
    b - *Watergate break-in, Washington, D.C.*
    c - *Largest U.S. drug deal in New York*

208. Who was a chairman of the Student Nonviolent Coordinating Committee?

    a - *Stokely Carmichael*
    b - *James Meredith*
    c - *Angela Davis*

209. What U.S. president appointed Andrew Young U.S. ambassador to the United Nations?

    a - *Jimmy Carter*
    b - *Ronald Reagan*
    c - *Gerald Ford*

210. In what year did the U.S. Supreme Court outlaw segregation of dining cars in *Henderson v. United States*?

    a - *1930*
    b - *1940*
    c - *1950*

211. In what year did the U.S. Supreme Court order school integration "with all deliberate speed"?

    a - *1945*
    b - *1955*
    c - *1959*

212. What amendment prohibits the requirement of a poll tax or any other tax for the privilege to vote?

    a - *Fifteenth*
    b - *Sixteenth*
    c - *Twenty-fourth*

213. What was the significance of the 1955 Bandung Conference?

    a - *Strategy meeting of civil rights leaders*
    b - *Meeting of leaders of colored nations of Africa and Asia*
    c - *Meeting to partition Africa*

214. Southern states held down the number of African American voters by issuing what was called the:

    a - *Southern Clause*
    b - *Grandfather Clause*
    c - *Confederate Clause*

215. Who were John Horse and John Caesar?

    a - *Black cowboys*
    b - *Black Union soldiers*
    c - *Black Indians who lived with the Seminole*

216. What did the Civil Rights Act of 1957 do?

    a - *Outlawed segregation*
    b - *Established a civil rights commission and a civil rights division in the Department of Justice*
    c - *Denied federal funds to schools that refused to integrate*

217. In 1955, the Interstate Commerce Commission banned segregation in:

    a - *Waiting rooms*
    b - *Buses*
    c - *All of the above*

218. What African American leader championed black nationalism and built a strong alliance between Africans and African Americans?

    a - *Martin Luther King, Jr.*
    b - *Ralph Abernathy*
    c - *Malcolm X*

With an uncompromising dedication to promoting the interests of women and minorities, Carol Moseley-Braun overcame the odds to become the first black woman elected to the U.S. Senate.

219. Who started the anti–Booker T. Washington campaign that led to the "Niagara Movement" and the NAACP?

    a - *William Trotter*
    b - *Walter White*
    c - *Frederick Douglass*

220. The first president of the National Association of Colored Women was:

    a - *Mary Church Terrell*
    b - *Sojourner Truth*
    c - *Mary McLeod Bethune*

221. What theologian and preacher was considered one of the great spiritual influences of this century, even affecting Martin Luther King, Jr.'s nonviolent beliefs?

    a - *Marcus Garvey*
    b - *Howard Thurman*
    c - *Elijah Muhammad*

222. In what year was Robert Weaver sworn in as the first black secretary of housing and urban development?

    a - *1926*
    b - *1966*
    c - *1992*

223. As register of the U.S. Treasury Department, whose signature appeared on every piece of U.S. paper money printed?

    a - *Blanche K. Bruce*
    b - *William H. Hastie*
    c - *Adam Clayton Powell, Jr.*

224. The first African American elected to Congress was:

    a - *Oscar D. Priest*
    b - *Blanche K. Bruce*
    c - *Hiram Revels*

225. (True or False) Benjamin Banneker assisted in the survey of Washington, D.C.

226. Who founded the Southern Christian Leadership Conference?

    a - *Stokely Carmichael*
    b - *Jesse Jackson*
    c - *Martin Luther King, Jr.*

227. In 1955 what 14-year-old boy was brutally murdered in Mississippi because he allegedly whistled at a white woman?

    a - *Medgar Evers*
    b - *Emmett Till*
    c - *James Chaney*

228. Who formed a new Nation of Islam after Elijah Muhammad's death?

    a - *W. D. Fard*
    b - *Malcolm X*
    c - *Louis Farrakhan*

229. Who was the first black to win a Nobel Prize in a category other than peace?

    a - *Toni Morrison*
    b - *Sir Arthur Lewis*
    c - *Bishop Desmond Tutu*

230. What was the first black school to establish undergraduate, graduate, and professional schools?

    a - *Morehouse College*
    b - *Fisk University*
    c - *Howard University*

231. What does ANC stand for?

    a - *African Nationalist Committee*
    b - *African National Congress*
    c - *American Negro Congress*

232. Who ruled the "separate but equal" doctrine invalid in 1954?

    a - *U.S. Congress*
    b - *U.S. Senate*
    c - *U.S. Supreme Court*

233. What was the name of the system in which African Americans farmed someone else's land and received a portion of the season's crop?

    a - *Slavery*
    b - *Barter*
    c - *Sharecropping*

234. What was the famous "Scottsboro case"?

    a - *Trial of 9 whites accused of lynching a black man*
    b - *Trial of 9 blacks accused of raping 2 white women*
    c - *Trial that used death penalty sentence for the first time*

235. The first African American mayor of Philadelphia was:

    a - *Maynard Jackson*
    b - *Harold Washington*
    c - *W. Wilson Goode*

236. Who said, "If a race has no history, . . . it becomes a negligible factor in the thought of the world, and it stands in danger of being exterminated"?

    a - *Malcolm X*
    b - *Carter G. Woodson*
    c - *Booker T. Washington*

237. (True or False) Booker T. Washington almost single-handedly created the *Journal of Negro History*.

A messenger of peace and social justice, Asa Philip Randolph was a relentless champion of the labor movement and a guiding light of the civil rights movement.

238. John H. Johnson is a distinguished:

    a - *Scholar*
    b - *Diplomat*
    c - *Publisher*

239. Who founded the DuSable Museum of African American History, located in Chicago, Illinois?

    a - *Dr. Margaret Burroughs*
    b - *W. E. B. Du Bois*
    c - *Mary McLeod Bethune*

240. What lawyer played a key role in the legal struggle that led to the *Brown v. Board of Education of Topeka* decision?

    a - *James Weldon Johnson*
    b - *Adam Clayton Powell*
    c - *Charles Hamilton Houston*

241. What U.S. president ended segregation in the U.S. Armed Forces by issuing an executive order?

   a - *Franklin D. Roosevelt*
   b - *Dwight D. Eisenhower*
   c - *Harry S. Truman*

242. What was one of Mary (Stagecoach Mary) Field's jobs in the old West?

   a - *Nurse*
   b - *Mail carrier*
   c - *Schoolteacher*

243. In what famous court case did the justices rule that, "Blacks are an inferior class of beings who had no rights which the white man was bound to respect"?

   a - *Brown v. Board of Education*
   b - *Sweatt v. Painter*
   c - *Dred Scott case*

244. Who founded an economic program called "People United to Save Humanity"?

   a - *W. E. B. Du Bois*
   b - *Ralph Abernathy*
   c - *Jesse Jackson*

245. (True or False) Ralph Bunche was the first African American recipient of a Nobel Prize.

246. What term referred to the large black population in the southern cotton growing states?

   a - *Cotton Belt*
   b - *Slave States*
   c - *Black Belt*

247. (True or False) The National Urban League was established strictly for the benefit of African Americans.

248. What U.S. president developed a coalition of African American advisers called the Black Cabinet?

   a - *Franklin D. Roosevelt*
   b - *Dwight D. Eisenhower*
   c - *John F. Kennedy*

249. What was the significance of Solidarity Day?

    a - *Labor union strike*
    b - *Multicultural education project*
    c - *Labor and civil rights protest of Reagan administration policies*

250. (True or False) In 1977 a record number of viewers, approximately 130 million, watched the television miniseries *Roots.*

251. When did the Supreme Court rule that busing was an acceptable way of integrating public schools?

    a - *1955*
    b - *1968*
    c - *1971*

252. The National Rainbow Coalition was organized to:

    a - *Unite people of all races and ethnicities*
    b - *Lobby for multicultural education*
    c - *Campaign for Jesse Jackson's presidential bid*

253. Andrew Hatcher was named associate press secretary to what U.S. president?

    a - *Lyndon B. Johnson*
    b - *Dwight D. Eisenhower*
    c - *John F. Kennedy*

254. The first African American governor since Reconstruction, L. Douglas Wilder, was elected in what state in 1989?

    a - *Maryland*
    b - *Virginia*
    c - *Michigan*

255. (True or False) Frederick Douglass and Martin R. Delany founded *The North Star,* an antislavery newspaper.

256. Who won the Nobel Peace Prize in 1984?

    a - *Jesse Jackson*
    b - *Nelson Mandela*
    c - *Bishop Desmond Tutu*

257. Who was refused admission to the University of Mississippi in 1961, forcing U.S. marshals to escort him to class?

   a - *Stokely Carmichael*
   b - *Ralph Abernathy*
   c - *James Meredith*

258. (True or False) On January 6, 1863, the Second Baptist Church in Detroit held an emancipation celebration, the first such celebration to follow Lincoln's proclamation.

259. By 1970, approximately 3 to 4 million African Americans attended integrated schools. Approximately how many African Americans attended integrated schools in 1960?

   a - *235,000*
   b - *543,000*
   c - *1.1 million*

260. (True or False) The Civil Rights Bill passed in 1866 ended slavery.

261. Whose innovative beauty products were sold throughout the United States and the Caribbean?

   a - *Madam C. J. Walker*
   b - *Lillian Dan*
   c - *Marie Convent*

262. What African American lawyer battled segregation in the military and the racist poll tax in the South?

   a - *William H. Hastie*
   b - *Thurgood Marshall*
   c - *Clarence Thomas*

263. Who was the first accredited African American physician in the United States?

   a - *James Derham*
   b - *Bernard Hughes*
   c - *Helen Dickens*

264. Who founded this nation's first major African American nationalist movement?

   a - *Marcus Garvey*
   b - *Malcolm X*
   c - *Frederick Douglass*

265. (True or False) Tom Bradley is the first African American to be elected mayor of Los Angeles for four terms.

266. In what year did John Sweat Rock practice before the Supreme Court?

    a - *1800*
    b - *1865*
    c - *1903*

267. In what city was Malcolm X assassinated?

    a - *Chicago*
    b - *New York*
    c - *Atlanta*

268. Who was the first African American chosen to lead a major political party (in 1989)?

    a - *Ron Brown*
    b - *Barbara Jordan*
    c - *Jesse Jackson*

269. In 1963 in Chicago, what did students participating in Freedom Day do?

    a - *Write essays on anniversary of Emancipation Proclamation*
    b - *March in support of southern civil rights movement*
    c - *Boycott school to protest de facto segregation*

270. Who was the first elected African American governor?

    a - *Maynard Jackson*
    b - *L. Douglas Wilder*
    c - *Harold Washington*

271. What African American sparked the "Montgomery Bus Boycott"?

    a - *Rosa Parks*
    b - *Martin Luther King, Jr.*
    c - *Ralph Abernathy*

272. In 1919 who did the U.S. State Department label "the most dangerous Negro in America" because of his determined opposition to racism?

    a - *A. Philip Randolph*
    b - *W. E. B. Du Bois*
    c - *Marcus Garvey*

As a conductor on the Underground Railroad, Harriet Tubman boldly risked her life time and again for the antislavery cause by leading slaves to freedom, nursing them to health, and acting as a spy for the Union army.

273. What was the first black-owned company to be listed on the American Stock Exchange?

    a - *Beatrice Foods*
    b - *Johnson Products, Co.*
    c - *Walker Hair Care Products*

274. Who was the first African American ever appointed to a federal judgeship?

    a - *Thurgood Marshall*
    b - *William H. Hastie*
    c - *Blanche K. Bruce*

275. In what year was Dr. Martin Luther King, Jr., assassinated?

    a - *1965*
    b - *1968*
    c - *1972*

276. Who was the first African American to have a seat on the New York Stock Exchange?

   a - *Joseph L. Searles*
   b - *Oscar D. Priest*
   c - *Carl Stokes*

277. Martin Luther King, Jr., graduated from what college?

   a - *Atlanta University*
   b - *Morehouse College*
   c - *Talladega College*

278. Who served as director of minority affairs for President Franklin D. Roosevelt?

   a - *Rufus Clement*
   b - *Mary McLeod Bethune*
   c - *Charles Johnson*

279. (True or False) The first two rap records were "King Tim III (Personality Jock)" by the Fatback Band and "Rapper's Delight" by the Sugar Hill Gang in 1975.

280. Who was this country's first African American general?

   a - *Colin Powell*
   b - *Benjamin O. Davis, Sr.*
   c - *Robert Smalls*

281. When did Jackie Robinson join the Brooklyn Dodgers, becoming the first African American player in the modern major leagues?

   a - *1940*
   b - *1947*
   c - *1951*

282. When did Jesse Jackson run for president of the United States?

   a - *1980 and 1984*
   b - *1984 and 1988*
   c - *1988 and 1992*

283. Who became the first African American woman president, calling herself "sister president" of Spelman College in 1987?

   a - *Lucy Craft Laney*
   b - *Johnnetta Betsch Cole*
   c - *Charlotte Brown*

284. Who was the first African American four-star general in U.S. military history?

    a - *Colin Powell*
    b - *Daniel James, Jr.*
    c - *Robert Smalls*

285. In what year did Macon B. Allen become the first African American lawyer?

    a - *1845*
    b - *1885*
    c - *1925*

286. Who was the first African American woman elected to the House of Representatives?

    a - *Shirley Chisholm*
    b - *Barbara Jordan*
    c - *Fannie Lou Hamer*

287. Who was the first African American to head the National Security Council?

    a - *Ron Brown*
    b - *Colin Powell*
    c - *Blanche K. Bruce*

288. Who led voter registration efforts in Mississippi in the late 1950s?

    a - *Ralph Abernathy*
    b - *Medgar Evers*
    c - *Malcolm X*

289. Who was called the "First Lady of Civil Rights"?

    a - *Fannie Lou Hamer*
    b - *Sojourner Truth*
    c - *Harriet Tubman*

290. Who was responsible for the program that organized special night classes to teach newly freed slaves?

    a - *Fanny Coppin*
    b - *Sojourner Truth*
    c - *Mary McLeod Bethune*

291. Who was the first African American to seek the presidential nomination of a major party?

    a - *Jesse Jackson*
    b - *Shirley Chisholm*
    c - *Julian Bond*

Lifting himself up from slavery to become the nation's most influential African American spokesman, Booker T. Washington built the Tuskegee Institute into America's largest and best-endowed black institution.

292. What is the name of the sculpture designed as a tribute to the four black girls killed during a church bombing in Alabama in 1963?

    a - *The Crucifixion*
    b - *Four Innocents*
    c - *Birmingham Tribute*

293. Who was the first notable churchman to preach that God is black?

    a - *Richard Allen*
    b - *Henry McNeal Turner*
    c - *Elijah Muhammad*

294. What navy mess attendant, a noncombatant with no training in operating guns, shot down four enemy planes in the Japanese attack on Pearl Harbor and became the first American hero of W.W. II?

    a - *Benjamin O. Davis, Jr.*
    b - *Dorie Miller*
    c - *Edward Brooke*

295. Who was the first African American to win an Oscar?

    a - *Hattie McDaniel*
    b - *Sidney Poitier*
    c - *Dorothy Dandridge*

296. Who first called for a protest march on Washington in 1941?

    a - *W. E. B. Du Bois*
    b - *A. Philip Randolph*
    c - *Roy Wilkins*

297. Where did Patrick Francis Healy become the first black president of a predominantly white university in 1871?

    a - *Georgetown University*
    b - *Columbia University*
    c - *Oberlin College*

298. Who published the first African American medical journal in 1892?

    a - *Miles Vandahurst Lynk*
    b - *John Russwurm*
    c - *John Johnson*

299. Who was the first accredited African American woman dentist in America?

    a - *Dr. Rebecca Cole*
    b - *Dr. Susan Stewart*
    c - *Dr. Ida Gray*

300. Who were the Freedom Riders?

    a - *Leaders of a slave revolt*
    b - *Interracial group riding through the South to test compliance with integration orders*
    c - *Leaders of the Underground Railroad*

301. Who has the best-selling album of all time?

    a - *Diana Ross*
    b - *Michael Jackson*
    c - *Quincy Jones*

302. Who coordinated Operation Desert Storm?

    a - *Benjamin O. Davis, Jr.*
    b - *Colin Powell*
    c - *Mike Espy*

303. In what year was civil rights leader Medgar Evers assassinated?

    a - *1963*
    b - *1968*
    c - *1890*

304. What NAACP official during the 1920s and '30s specialized in investigating lynchings and race riots?

    a - *W. E. B. Du Bois*
    b - *Walter White*
    c - *Roy Wilkins*

305. Who was the founder of the Universal Negro Industrial Association?

    a - *Marcus Garvey*
    b - *A. Philip Randolph*
    c - *Martin Luther King, Jr.*

306. Who organized the Poor People's Campaign in Washington, D.C., after the assassination of Martin Luther King, Jr.?

    a - *Reverend Ralph Abernathy*
    b - *Jesse Jackson*
    c - *Julian Bond*

307. Who was the first black woman to have a non-stereotypical role in her own television series?

    a - *Oprah Winfrey*
    b - *Diahann Carroll*
    c - *Cicely Tyson*

308. Who is known as the Mother of the Civil Rights struggle in California?

    a - *Angela Davis*
    b - *Mary Ellen Pleasant*
    c - *Ida Wells-Barnett*

309. What doctor attended President James Garfield after he was shot?

    a - *Dr. Charles Purvis*
    b - *Dr. Charles Drew*
    c - *Dr. Roland Scott*

310. Who built San Francisco's first hotel and opened California's first public school?

    a - *Madam C. J. Walker*
    b - *Maggie Lena Walker*
    c - *William Leidesdorff*

311. What Chicago abolitionist led a 12-year campaign to abolish the Illinois laws that denied African Americans the right to vote?

    a - *Harold Washington*
    b - *John Jones*
    c - *Jean Baptiste Pointe DuSable*

312. Who was responsible for securing equal rights for black troops during the Civil War?

    a - *Marcus Garvey*
    b - *George T. Downing*
    c - *Frederick Douglass*

313. Who made a speech at the National Negro Convention in 1843 that made people regard him as one of the most militant abolitionists?

    a - *Booker T. Washington*
    b - *Frederick Douglass*
    c - *Rev. Henry Garnet*

314. What African American was a vice presidential candidate at the 1968 Democratic National Convention?

    a - *Julian Bond*
    b - *Jesse Jackson*
    c - *Stokely Carmichael*

315. At the urging of Walter White, what president issued a landmark executive order to practice fair hiring practices in federal agencies?

    a - *Lyndon B. Johnson*
    b - *John F. Kennedy*
    c - *Harry S. Truman*

316. Who is known as the Father of Negro History?

    a - *Carter G. Woodson*
    b - *Langston Hughes*
    c - *Richard Wright*

317. Who was the first African American to be appointed as a member of the United States delegation to the United Nations?

    a - *Thurgood Marshall*
    b - *Paul Robeson*
    c - *Edith Sampson*

318. Who was known as the "Black Edison"?

    a - *Granville T. Woods*
    b - *Lewis Latimer*
    c - *Lloyd Hall*

319. In 1990 the first black news anchor team in a major metropolitan area was on a CBS affiliate in:

    a - *Atlanta*
    b - *New York City*
    c - *Philadelphia*

320. What religious group played a large role in the abolition movement?

    a - *Quakers*
    b - *Catholics*
    c - *Baptists*

321. Who was the spiritual leader of the Nation of Islam?

    a - *Malcolm X*
    b - *Elijah Muhammad*
    c - *Martin Luther King, Jr.*

322. Who was Martin Luther King, Jr.'s executive assistant?

    a - *Ralph Abernathy*
    b - *Jesse Jackson*
    c - *Wyatt Tee Walker*

323. What post–Civil War president allowed the ex-Confederate states to form governments that completely excluded African Americans from the political process?

    a - *Andrew Johnson*
    b - *Grover Cleveland*
    c - *Ulysses S. Grant*

324. The word "carpetbagger" was first used during the aftermath of what war?

    a - *Revolutionary War*
    b - *World War I*
    c - *Civil War*

325. Who urged America to "keep hope alive"?

    a - *Malcolm X*
    b - *Jesse Jackson*
    c - *Martin Luther King, Jr.*

ANSWERS

1. a   **March to Selma**
2. c   **"I Have a Dream"**
3.   **True**
4. b   **Ralph Abernathy**
5. a   **the *North Star***
6. a   **Tuskegee Institute**
7.   **True**
8. a   **"There are no good times to be black in America, but some times are worse than others."**
9. c   **1865**
10.   **True**
11. a   **Jean Baptiste Pointe DuSable**
12. b   **Barbara Jordan**
13. b   **Harriet Tubman**
14. c   **Malcolm X**
15. b   **1837**
16. a   **P. B. S. Pinchback**
17.   **False - W. D. Fard**
18. a   **NAACP**
19. b   **Florida**
20. a   **Huey P. Newton & Bobby Seale**
21. b   **Carl Stokes in Cleveland**
22. a   **Jane Addams & William Dean Howells**
23. a   **Walter Mosley**
24. c   **John Roy Lynch**
25. c   **Iraq**
26. a   **Congress of Racial Equality**
27. c   **Andrew Young**
28. b   **Colin Powell**
29. c   **Paul Cuffe**
30. b   **Ida B. Wells-Barnett**
31. b   **National Association for the Advancement of Colored People**
32. a   **Thurgood Marshall**
33. b   **Information Agency**
34. b   **Malcolm X**
35. b   **Booker T. Washington**
36. c   **Alain Locke**

37. b **Charlotte E. Ray**
38. b **189,000**
39. b **70,000**
40. a **Civil War**
41. **False - National Association of Colored Women**
42. c **Negro History Week**
43. b **1 million**
44. **True**
45. a **Mary McLeod Bethune**
46. a **Give each 40 acres and a mule**
47. b **William H. Carney**
48. b **Toni Morrison**
49. **False - Swayne Hall, Talladega College**
50. **True**
51. b **Civil rights leader**
52. a **Character in popular minstrel shows of the 19th century**
53. a *Mitchell vs. U.S. Interstate Commerce Act*
54. **True**
55. a **1619**
56. **True**
57. **True**
58. a *Rainbow*
59. c **Sharon Pratt Kelly**
60. b **Lenora Fulani**
61. **True**
62. c **Alabama**
63. a **Dexter Avenue Baptist Church**
64. b **Maggie Lena Walker**
65. **True**
66. c *Brown v. Board of Education of Topeka*
67. **True**
68. b **39**
69. b **1968**
70. a **Indentured servants**
71. a **1,000 per year**
72. **True**
73. c **Muhammad Ali**
74. b **Barbara Jordan**
75. **True**
76. a **James Baldwin**
77. a **Malcolm X**
78. **True**
79. a **Organizing a slave revolt**
80. c **A. Philip Randolph**
81. **True**
82. **True**
83. b **385,000**
84. c **Any means necessary to fight slavery**
85. c **Maria W. Stewart**

86. a They were offered freedom
87.   False - Ralph Ellison
88. c Atlanta
89. a Richard Allen
90. a Crispus Attucks
91. c Ida B. Wells-Barnett
92. c Jim Crow
93. c 3 million
94.   False - Harlem Renaissance
95. c Once every day or two
96. a Buffalo Soldiers
97.   True
98. a An African American nationalist
99.   False
100.   True
101.   False - Colorado
102.   True
103. b Clara Brown
104. c Colonists
105.   True
106. a Benjamin E. Mays
107. b 10,000
108. c 1976
109.   True
110. b William S. Whipper
111. c Paul Laurence Dunbar
112. b Township clerk and then U.S. Congress
113. a Hotel and restaurant owner
114. a Reaching the North Pole first
115. a One of the first African American millionaires
116.   False - Dr. Carter G. Woodson
117. b Association for the Study of Negro Life and History
118. c Booker T. Washington
119.   True
120. a Adam Clayton Powell, Jr.
121. b The Red Summer
122. b Hiram Revels
123. c John Brown
124. a Benjamin Harrison
125.   False - Asked him to resign
126. a Milton Olive
127. a Grand Central Station
128. a Countee Cullen, Langston Hughes, Zora Neale Hurston
129. c Prince Hall
130. b Andrew Bryan
131. b Lyndon B. Johnson
132. a John Russwurm
133. b Coretta Scott King

134. a Pony Express riders
135. b Blacks were not U.S. citizens and therefore had no rights
136. a 1861
137. b Made African Americans citizens
138. b Children's Defense Fund
139. a Paul Robeson
140. c 1993
141. a Joseph H. Rainey
142.   True
143. b Absalom Jones
144. b Prince Hall
145.   False - Approved
146. c Vermont
147.   True
148. b William Tucker
149. a Massachusetts
150.   True
151. c Chicago
152. c Senate
153. a Ralph Bunche
154. b Bobby Rush
155. c Martin Luther King, Jr.
156. b World War II
157.   True
158. b Ernest Everett Just
159. b Jack Johnson
160. c Fifteenth
161.   True
162. b Underground Railroad
163.   False - He was born a slave
164.   False - Denied African Americans their rights
165. b John Brown
166.   True
167.   True
168. a "Atlanta Compromise"
169.   False - *The Color Purple*
170. c One year
171. a President of the NAACP
172.   True
173. c Pennsylvania State House of Representatives
174. a Jane M. Bolin
175. a Banned the "white primary" that prevented blacks in the South from voting
176. b S.S. *Frederick Douglass*
177. c The first African American woman federal judge
178. b Anna Deavere Smith
179. a 1954
180. a Controlled by slave mutineers
181. a Thirteenth

182.   **True**
183. c **Fugitive Slave Act**
184. b **Spied**
185.   **False - Robert Abbott, editor of the *Chicago Defender***
186. c **Angela Davis**
187. c **Gordon Parks**
188. a **Harry Belafonte**
189. b **Missouri Compromise**
190.   **False - Black preacher with a white congregation**
191. a **Robert Weaver**
192. c **300**
193. c **Joycelyn Elders**
194. b **Thurgood Marshall**
195. c **Mayor**
196. b **Governor George Wallace**
197. c **Ghana**
198. a **All have been executive secretary of the NAACP**
199. b **Guion Bluford, Jr.**
200. c **Denied federal funds to any state that practiced segregation**
201. c **To withdraw U.S. investments in South Africa to protest apartheid**
202. c **Potato chip**
203. b **1925**
204.   **True**
205. a **1820**
206. a **1850**
207. b **Watergate break-in, Washington, D.C.**
208. a **Stokely Carmichael**
209. a **Jimmy Carter**
210. c **1950**
211. b **1955**
212. c **Twenty-fourth**
213. b **Meeting of leaders of colored nations of Africa and Asia**
214. b **Grandfather Clause**
215. c **Black Indians who lived with the Seminole**
216. b **Established a civil rights commission and a civil rights division in the Department of Justice**
217. c **All of the above**
218. c **Malcolm X**
219. a **William Trotter**
220. a **Mary Church Terrell**
221. b **Howard Thurman**
222. b **1966**
223. a **Blanche K. Bruce**
224. c **Hiram Revels**
225.   **True**
226. c **Martin Luther King, Jr.**
227. b **Emmett Till**

228. c **Louis Farrakhan**
229. b **Sir Arthur Lewis (in economics)**
230. c **Howard University**
231. b **African National Congress**
232. c **U.S. Supreme Court**
233. c **Sharecropping**
234. b **Trial of 9 blacks accused of raping 2 white women**
235. c **W. Wilson Goode**
236. b **Carter G. Woodson**
237.   **False - Carter G. Woodson**
238. c **Publisher**
239. a **Dr. Margaret Burroughs**
240. c **Charles Hamilton Houston**
241. c **Harry S. Truman**
242. b **Mail carrier**
243. c **_Dred Scott_ case**
244. c **Jesse Jackson**
245.   **True**
246. c **Black Belt**
247.   **False - It was an interracial organization**
248. a **Franklin D. Roosevelt**
249. c **Labor and civil rights protest of Reagan administration policies**
250.   **True**
251. c **1971**
252. c **Campaign for Jesse Jackson's presidential bid**
253. c **John F. Kennedy**
254. b **Virginia**
255.   **True**
256. c **Bishop Desmond Tutu**
257. c **James Meredith**
258.   **True**
259. a **235,000**
260.   **False - Gave blacks full and equal benefit of all laws**
261. a **Madam C. J. Walker**
262. a **William H. Hastie**
263. a **James Derham**
264. a **Marcus Garvey**
265.   **True**
266. b **1865**
267. b **New York**
268. a **Ron Brown**
269. c **Boycott school to protest de facto segregation**
270. b **L. Douglas Wilder**
271. a **Rosa Parks**
272. a **Asa Philip Randolph**
273. b **Johnson Products, Co.**
274. b **William H. Hastie**
275. b **1968**
276. a **Joseph L. Searles**

277. b Morehouse College
278. b Mary McLeod Bethune
279.   False - 1979
280. b Benjamin O. Davis, Sr.
281. b 1947
282. b 1984 and 1988
283. b Johnnetta Betsch Cole
284. b Daniel James, Jr.
285. a 1845
286. a Shirley Chisholm
287. b Colin Powell
288. b Medgar Evers
289. a Fannie Lou Hamer
290. a Fanny Coppin
291. b Shirley Chisholm
292. a *The Crucifixion*
293. b Henry McNeal Turner
294. b Dorie Miller
295. a Hattie McDaniel
296. b Asa Philip Randolph
297. a Georgetown University
298. a Miles Vandahurst Lynk
299.   Dr. Ida Gray
300. b Interracial group riding through the South to
        test compliance with integration orders
301. b Michael Jackson
302. b Colin Powell
303. a 1963
304. b Walter White
305. a Marcus Garvey
306. a Reverend Ralph Abernathy
307. b Diahann Carroll
308. b Mary Ellen Pleasant
309. a Dr. Charles Purvis
310. c William Leidesdorff
311. b John Jones
312. b George T. Downing
313. c Rev. Henry Garnet
314. a Julian Bond
315. c Harry S. Truman
316. a Carter G. Woodson
317. c Edith Sampson
318. a Granville T. Woods
319. b New York City
320. a Quakers
321. b Elijah Muhammad
322. c Wyatt Tee Walker
323. a Andrew Johnson
324. c Civil War
325. b Jesse Jackson

INDEX

R. S. RENNERT has edited the nearly 100 volumes in Chelsea House's award-winning BLACK AMERICANS OF ACHIEVEMENT series, which tells the stories of black men and women who have helped shape the course of modern history, and the 10 volumes in the PROFILES OF GREAT BLACK AMERICANS series. He is also the author of several sports biographies, including *Henry Aaron, Jesse Owens,* and *Jackie Robinson.*